FIRST BOOK OF
BABY ANIMALS

David Roberts

Sundial

CONTENTS

Photographs at the front of this book:

(Endpapers) A rookery of King Penguin chicks on South Georgia in the Antarctic. It will be some time before the chicks lose their brown down and grow as tall as the adult penguins.

(Title pages) Cheetah mother and cub at rest but still alert on the East African savannah.

(Contents pages) A young Giant Panda chewing bamboo shoots, which are among its favourite food. This bear-like carnivore is a native of south-west China and is called by the Chinese, beishung, the white bear.

First published 1977 by
Sundial Books Limited
59 Grosvenor Street
London W1

© 1977 Hennerwood Publications Limited

ISBN 0 904230 50 3

Printed in Great Britain by Jarrold & Sons Limited, Norwich.

INTRODUCTION

All of us begin life as babies. We ought to know what it is like to be a baby. We ought to remember the shape and colour of the first balloon we ever saw, the shock it gave us when it burst with a bang. We ought to remember the smell and taste of our first jam tart and the sticky feeling it left on our fingers.

Why don't we? Perhaps it is because a baby has so much to learn, so much to remember. How it came to learn so much and remember so much is not important. We must all learn to walk, run, jump and climb. The struggles involved in our early achievements, the bumps, the falls, the failures are best forgotten.

Yet because what happened to us as

babies has made us what we are, because we may one day need to bring up babies of our own, we like to remember what we can about our babyhood. We like to think about our own early days, to talk about them to older people who do remember what we were like and, above all, to watch the behaviour of the babies we meet.

Other animals cannot do this. They cannot think as we do because they have no words with which to reason and to form their thoughts. They cannot discuss their own behaviour with others of their kind. They can only do what comes naturally to them. They are urged on to behave as they do by what we call their natural instincts.

It is astonishing what baby animals can learn, apparently with no one to teach them. Because they are more fully developed at birth and grow faster than human babies, they learn to do what they can do more quickly. The baby antelope can stand on its legs, walk and even run within hours of its birth. The farmyard chick can run about and feed itself almost as soon as it has left the egg.

Yet all animals are dependent upon one or other, or both, of their parents for their early survival. Egg-laying animals find ways to protect the eggs until they hatch. Spiders wrap them in parcels of silk. Turtles bury them in the sand. Birds build cunningly concealed nests for them and watch over them until they hatch.

Mammals also make nests or dig underground nurseries. They provide their babies with their first food from

cruelties in the family life of animals are essential to the process of growing up. It is a matter of urgency to learn the arts of survival.

We have learnt a lot from the family life of animals. Insects and birds have taught us to build shelters from the weather. Burrowing animals have taught us where to find hidden food and how to store food for the winter famine. Their breeding habits have taught us how to produce new breeds of animals, better suited to our own needs or the tasks we have trained them to do for us.

As keepers, employers, exploiters, masters and the most dangerous competitors of the whole animal kingdom, we bear a great responsibility towards them. As we crowd them out of the limited space available on our planet, we must learn how they live and rear their young. We will then know how better to leave them alone to live their own lives in a way that suits them.

On the pages of this book you will meet many of the world's babies, perhaps for the first time. They may remind you what it was like to be a baby yourself.

their own bodies and share their own food with them. As they grow older, the youngsters are often taught to hunt and kill their own food. Elephant mothers continue to suckle their young many years beyond their babyhood.

Most baby animals are happy to explore and learn from their natural environment. When they are not, the parents resort to force. The otter and the water vole thrust their reluctant offspring into the water so that they must learn to swim or drown. The young of many animals are abandoned by their parents as soon as they are old enough to fend for themselves. Many of the apparent

PETS

Keeping pets is most fascinating when you start with the baby animal and watch over its growing up. Dogs, in particular, enjoy living with people. They will learn your funny ways just as you learn theirs. In return for food and companionship, they have been willing to help people with their hunting and herding of other domestic animals. It seems that some dogs never realise they are dogs at all, but think of themselves as smaller members of your family.

Other pets do not abandon their wild ways so easily. To be happy, they need to live as nearly as possible in the way they would in the wild. This means that they should be given the privacy you often want for yourself. Once they have the food and comforts their kind is used to, they will become interested in your life, too, and tame enough to allow you to join them in their games.

► Cats can settle down comfortably to life in your home, but they never quite abandon all their wild ways. A kitten's play is often practice for the hunting it would need to do to survive in the wild. Learn to play your kitten's games, if you want to be friends.

Siamese kittens are born white all over. Their colour 'points' on ears, nose and paws appear gradually. There are seven recognised breeds: Seal Point, Chocolate Point, Blue Point, Lilac Point, Tabby Point (sometimes called Lynx Point), Red Point and Tortie Point. These are Seal Point kittens. Fully-grown, Siamese have triangular faces, long, lean bodies, long, whiplike tails, and hindlegs slightly higher than forelegs. Their eyes are a distinctive deep blue. The Siamese Cat Club was founded in 1901 and has a championship show in London in the autumn every year.

The Tabby kitten is born with the familiar, tigerlike markings, though sometimes they fade in the first weeks to reappear later. Brown, Silver and Red are the recognised breeds of the long-haired tabby; Red, Brown and Silver are the short-haired varieties. The distinctive M-mark on the forehead of all tabbies is said to be where the prophet Mahomet touched his favourite cat to give it his blessing. The other markings, so the legend goes, were made by his fingers stroking his pet. These markings can be either striped or in whorls giving the shoulders a butterfly-wing pattern.

Wolves crept up to the ancient hunter's campfire, lured by the scraps and bones he threw away. At least 10,000 years ago, the first orphan cubs were reared as pets and to help the hunter in the chase. With the change of diet and habits, they gradually evolved doglike characteristics. Since then, varieties have been bred that resemble their wolf ancestors hardly at all. For instance, these Beagle pups have been bred as hunting dogs. They look lively enough here, but they are born almost helpless. At three weeks, they can stand and follow their mother. At two months, they are weaned and fending for themselves.

Like children, kittens have a great deal of curiosity. By the time they are old enough to leave their mothers, they have become naturally wary. When an interesting object is spotted, they will often approach it in a roundabout way. This kitten has crept up on the wind-fluttering grass from behind a fence. Cats, unlike most animals, depend more on their remarkable senses of sight and hearing, rather than smell, when they go hunting. This kitten, ears pricked, eyes concentrating and paw reaching for its 'prey', is practising the hunting arts.

14

▲ From the start, long-haired kittens
need daily grooming to get rid of
tangles and loose hairs. Grooming
themselves, they may swallow so much
hair that a furball forms in the tummy,
sometimes needing surgery to remove it.
All kittens are born with blue eyes, like
those of this Long-haired Black. The
White's eyes have changed to orange.

Pet guinea-pigs have been bred in all sorts of colours. They can be plain white or a mottled brown, black or glowing orange. In their natural home, the northern part of the South American continent, wild guinea-pigs are usually reddish-brown. They were first brought to Europe by Dutch explorers in the 16th century and soon became popular with children. The babies are born with wide-open eyes, bright and curious from the start. Within an hour of birth, they are running about quite actively. In a week or so, they have grown, like this one, to about a third the size of the mother. The usual litter is between one and four babies, weaned after about three weeks.

The eyes of this Tabby kitten are just beginning to change from the blue they were when they first opened to the green of the adult cat. The pricked ears are like bowls to collect the smallest sounds, and the keen eyes pick up the smallest movement. Tabby is on the prowl, practising the silent approach of the hunter through the long grass. Pet kittens should be given plenty of space to explore where they cannot come to harm. They soon learn to climb and rarely hurt themselves in a fall. But make allowances for their intense curiosity and avoid letting them near sharp objects or containers that can be upset. Tree-climbing is good for keeping their claws well trimmed.

◀ Kittens should not be removed from the mother until at least eight weeks old when they have been properly weaned. Even then, a kitten brought into a new household will miss the companionship of the litter. This is a time when it will best make friends with other pets. The phrase: 'fighting like cat and dog' has little truth in it. They are not natural enemies. When both animals are well fed and without jealousy of each other, they can become the best of chums, like this contented couple.

▼ This English Cocker Spaniel pup belongs to one of the most popular breeds. When choosing from a litter, avoid one that is shy and hides from you in the corner. Always pick a bright and friendly one. This rule applies to all breeds. A frightened puppy can grow into a dangerous dog, and even puppies can give a sharp bite. English Cocker Spaniels can be jealous, so make sure he is equally friendly with all members of the family. They need plenty of handling and human contact from an early age.

Females of the rodent family are caring mothers and make interesting pets to breed. The rabbit mother, the doe, should be given plenty of hay to build a nest, which she will line with fur from her own body. Newly born rabbits are blind, deaf and almost naked. They need the warmth of the nest and the mother for their first two weeks. Their eyes open after about eleven days. By the end of the two weeks, they begin to leave the nest and to eat solid food. In the wild, they would be born at the end of a short burrow called a 'stop' or 'stob', leaving it when their sight and hearing have developed and they are covered with warm, soft fur. Pet baby rabbits should be given plenty of space to move about in a wired-in run as soon as they are able.

Another rodent that has become a popular pet in recent years is the gerbil or sand rat from the desert and semi-desert regions of Africa and Asia. The large eyes show that it is an animal mostly active at night. The mother should be given a dark place to build her nest and give birth to a litter of about eight babies. In the wild, the babies remain in an underground burrow for about three weeks. When they first venture out after three weeks, they are miniature versions of the mother. Here, mother and baby touch noses outside the hidden burrow.

Here is a litter of gerbils still in the nest. Their eyes have not yet opened, and they huddle together for warmth and comfort. The mother has come to visit them after a foraging trip to the upper world under cover of darkness. Already, the babies have their mother's colouring and markings. If danger threatens, she will carry them one by one to a safer hiding place.

▼ This Beagle puppy and
Long-haired Red kitten eye each
other a bit warily. If they continue to live
together, they ought to become the best
of friends. It is usually owners who
create the enmity between cats and
dogs. Left to themselves, they will enjoy
each other's company. Beagles, bred as
hunting dogs, must be given plenty of
exercise. The Long-haired Red or Red
Persian is rather rare, as it is not easy to
breed without tabby markings that
would disqualify it for showing. This
kitten should grow into a winner.

In 1930, a female golden hamster and her litter of twelve babies were dug out of their burrow near Aleppo in Syria and taken to the Hebrew University in Jerusalem. Since then, all the pet golden hamsters in the world have descended from that one family, including the happy mother and young in the picture. No other golden hamsters have been found in the wild, and the wild animal is believed to be extinct. Hamsters sleep through most of the winter, waking for an occasional feed. Adult hamsters should be kept separately.

The Goldfish or Golden Carp is a freshwater fish from China and Japan. In the wild state it is brown, the gold colour having been bred into the domesticated species. Babies, like those in the picture, are a bronze colour which turns to gold as they grow older. In Japan, breeders have produced many different varieties, such as the Pop-eye, the Veil-tail and the Lion-head.

▲ The hunting instincts of a well-fed kitten have little chance to develop but its curiosity remains as keen as ever. In the familiar surroundings of its own home, it may have nothing to fear, but every newcomer must be examined. The slow, silent movements of the snail fascinate this kitten. Once it has shown that it is no threat to the kitten, it can be ignored. The kitten shows acceptance by washing itself.

▶ All members of the cat family like to have their own marked-out territory. A kitten's curiosity is partly the serious business of checking its territory for changes and interlopers. When it knows there is nothing to fear, it is content to settle down for the frequent snoozes the growing animal needs. It will accept its own blanket-lined basket as its lair, settling there happily between bouts of play.

All pets in the same household should meet each other as soon as possible and never unexpectedly. This fully-grown guinea-pig senses that it has nothing to fear from the kitten. The kitten approaches it warily, uncertain whether it bites or not. Here, they have been introduced to each other in the open space of a lawn. Both of them have plenty of room to retreat. Once they are both sure they have nothing to quarrel about, they will accept each other and live happily together.

It is not always easy to tell what breed puppies are. This is a Bull Mastiff. As the name implies, it is a cross between a Bulldog and a Mastiff. The breed was first produced by gamekeepers to help them catch poachers. This puppy will grow to have the fighting qualities of the Bulldog, but will be as large and quick as a Mastiff. At one time, they were bred for a dark colouring, difficult to see in the dark. The lighter colour is preferred for today's pets.

This Dalmatian puppy is one of a breed that was once trained as carriage dogs. Long-legged and tireless, they trotted along behind a horse-drawn carriage and waited beside it on guard while the master paid a call. There are two kinds of Dalmatian, those with black spots and those with liver-coloured spots. In a well-bred Dalmatian, the spots should not be bigger than a large coin and should not merge together into patches. This pup, like all the breed, will be full of romping fun, enjoy human companionship and return it with lifelong loyalty.

This English Cocker Spaniel is worn out with play. Though still wide awake, it slumps down to rest its weary limbs. It looks as though it were very sorry for itself, but like all English Cocker Spaniels it is a happy pup with a sense of humour. The breed is one of the most popular as a pet, and these dogs are often trained as gundogs. They are ideal household pets as long as they are not spoiled.

Here is a pair of very proud-looking King Charles Spaniels. At one time, a favourite pet of royalty and nobility, this breed has been included in many famous paintings. Though not, nowadays, so popular as a pet, the King Charles Spaniel is an attractive animal with its distinctive domed head and appealing eyes. It is a later development from the older and larger variety, known as the Comforter in Elizabethan times, as is the modern Cavalier King Charles.

This is a family of rare mixed Cameo Long-haired kittens. Long-haired kittens are full of fun and very pretty. When they grow up, they will be quieter than most other cats. If they are groomed regularly, they will be quite content to sit about posing decoratively. There are altogether about twenty different colours. Eyes vary with orange, blue, green and even odd-eyed, one blue and one orange.

A kitten, weaned from its mother at eight weeks, needs then to be fed a little at a time and often. Three or four meals can be just milk with cereal and egg. At least twice a day, small quantities of raw beef or cooked meat should be given. Vary this with minced raw liver, cooked and boned fish or cooked rabbit. Reduce to four meals at twelve weeks and two at six months. Always supply water as well as milk.

There are eight varieties of dogs bred in Britain for herding sheep and cattle. The Old English, Shetland, Rough and Smooth coated Collies, the Border and Bearded Collies are used to herd sheep; the Cardigan and Pembroke Welsh Corgis are for cattle. Here is a Bearded Collie mother with her puppy. Bearded Collies have a double coat. The outer one is of long, straight hair from which water runs easily, keeping the dog dry. Underneath is a soft, woolly coat to keep it warm. Combing tends to pull out too much of the woolly undercoat, so a brush should always be used for grooming this breed.

◀ This Labrador pup is one of a breed originally trained as a retriever gundog. More importantly, nowadays, Labradors are the breed most often used as guide dogs for the blind. Bitches make the best guide dogs, because they are less likely to be distracted than male dogs. The dog is fitted with a special harness through which communication is made between animal and owner. Both have to go through training and to be carefully matched to each other. A strong bond grows up between them, giving a blind person great confidence and mobility.

▼ Here is another example of pets living happily together. The Pekinese, the rabbit and the cat get on well because they have no jealousy or fear of each other. It helps if the different animals are brought together when they are still babies. As they grow up together and are treated with equality by their owners, they take each other for granted. When a new pet is brought into the home where pets are already living, it should never be fussed over too much. Animals, like children, hate to be left out of things. Jealousies can grow among them, too.

◄ Burmese cats are getting to be almost as popular as Siamese. This Brown Burmese kitten's coat will darken as it grows older until it is a deep, glossy brown. This is the original colour for a Burmese and is sometimes called a Sable. New colours have been bred, such as the Red, Cream, Tortie, Chocolate, Blue Cream and Lilac, each very attractive in its way. The coat of a Burmese is very short with the hairs lying closely together. The head is a little less pointed than a Siamese's. Burmese are mischievous, but intelligent and easy to train. They also get on well with other cats and with dogs.

► These bright-looking youngsters are called bi-coloured kittens, meaning they have two colours. There are black and white, and red and white, both short-haired and long-haired, recognised as pedigree breeds. This means that they can win prizes in a cat show. There are more than sixty breeds recognised as different. This is not to suggest that pedigree cats make better pets. How a kitten is treated will decide how it behaves as a pet. If it is given care and love and played with at the games it likes best, it will repay its owners with good behaviour and return their love with plenty of interest.

If it is at all possible, kittens should be allowed to play out of doors. This will give them all sorts of new interests. They can behave like the little hunters they really are, stalking real or imaginary game through the long grass and among the bushes. They should be allowed to climb trees to keep their claws in trim, even fences so long as they do not wander into other gardens. They will enjoy chasing leaves and insects, meeting other animals and sniffing the hundreds of new scents surrounding them. Always remember that a kitten whose life is filled with interest will be a contented kitten.

These Basset puppies happily share the water in their drinking bowl. A bowl of clean, fresh water should always be available for your pet dog. Puppies are usually weaned from their mother's milk at about six weeks old. Then the puppy should be feeding itself. The bigger it grows, the more it will eat, of course. The amount will depend both on its size and the work it does during the day. The important thing is not to allow your pet to grow fat and lazy.

This West Highland White is a breed of terrier with a lot of character. He will make a delightful pet and will not grow too big for the average home. Before you rush out to buy a puppy just like him, or any pet for that matter, remember that an animal in the home is not in its natural surroundings. It cannot fend for itself as it would do in the wild. It depends on you for its health and happiness, for its survival even. Give it love, but don't spoil it. Teach it to behave in the home and out for a walk, but don't be harsh to it. A pet wants to settle into whatever surroundings it finds itself in and to get on with the business of living. Give it everything it needs, including the right to live its own life as naturally as possible. A contented pet will bring you rewards enough.

SMALL BABIES

Some baby animals are very small in comparison with their parents. Some are small because they have small parents. Nature has found many ways to protect small babies in their early lives. Some animals, like the marsupials of Australia and elsewhere, have pockets into which their babies can snuggle. Spiders wrap their eggs in parcels of silk to keep them warm and protected until the babies hatch out. Some parents build nests, some dig burrows and some use the natural protection of the foliage around them.

Egg-laying mothers often leave their eggs to hatch out by themselves and their babies to face the start of life on their own. Others watch over their babies as they grow, carrying them about with them and teaching them, by example, to look after themselves.

Everywhere, Nature's plans seem to work. The tiniest, the weakest and most helpless of new-born babies survive.

◄ The colugo is a kind of lemur with skinflaps stretched between its legs like wings. With these outspread, it can glide from branch to branch in its treetop home. A mother colugo climbs and glides with her baby clinging on.

▲ The cuscus or woolly phalanger is an animal of Australia and the East Indies. It is a marsupial, which means that the mother keeps her babies in a pouch while they are growing up. Her pouch is big enough to hold the two to four tiny, new-born young. They are ill-formed at first, but have room to grow while feeding from the mother's teats. This baby has grown too big for the pouch. It clings to its mother's fur with claws made for gripping, as she uses hers to clamber about her tree-top home. There are five different species of cuscus. This baby will grow, like its mother, to be about the size of a cat. The big eyes indicate an animal that is most active at night.

▶ Here is another kind of phalanger, the ring-tailed possum. Its name comes from its habit of curling its tail in a tight ring. It comes from New Guinea, Australia and Tasmania. The baby grew from its tiny beginnings in its mother's pouch, but now it clings on to her back. Tree-dwelling mammals like this need to move about a good deal among the branches in search of food. It is safer for the mother to carry her babies with her until they are old enough to fend for themselves. The large, bright eyes show how well the possum can see in the dark when this shy animal ventures out on its foraging expeditions. The photographer's bright lights have, for the moment, contracted the usually wide-open pupils.

▲ The koala bear, the cuddly teddy bear favourite from Australia, is not a bear at all but a kind of phalanger. Unlike other phalangers, the mother's pouch opens to the rear instead of forwards. Koala mothers carry their babies about until they are nearly as big as themselves. They will even look after another mother's baby. They have only one baby at a time, born not much more than 2 centimetres ($\frac{3}{4}$ inch) long. Fathers will rarely carry the growing youngster about with them.

► This agile wallaby is one of several species of wallabies from Australia, closely related to but smaller than the kangaroo. The new-born baby, barely 2 centimetres ($\frac{3}{4}$ inch) long, blind and almost helpless, takes three minutes to crawl into its mother's pouch. In three months, it is weaned and able to leave the pouch though it often returns there when it is tired or frightened. Babies like this one will hitch a ride even when the pouch has become a rather tight fit.

◄ The grey squirrel was introduced into Britain from North America and is now much more common than the native red squirrel. Squirrels build two kinds of nests. One is a storehouse and temporary shelter. The other, the winter 'drey', is used as a nursery. It is a dome of leafy twigs in the angle between the trunk of a tree and a branch, or sometimes in a hollow tree. It is lined with leaves, grass, moss and, when available, honeysuckle bark. The mother has two litters, in late winter and spring. This youngster was born blind, naked and helpless. As soon as it could see and had grown some warm fur, it ventured out of the drey. At first, its movements were jerky and hesitant. It soon learned to grip with its strong claws. As its tail grew more bushy, helping its balance, it became bolder. The weaning process, encouraging it to find its own food, soon had it scampering up and down the trunk, and leaping from branch to branch.

▲ The tree kangaroo is another marsupial from Australia and New Guinea. It lives in the trees of the tropical rain forest. It is similar to the ground-dwelling kangaroo, but its thick coat gives it a more bear-like appearance. Like its relatives, the baby is born very small and crawls into the forward facing pouch of its mother. There it is suckled until it grows too big for the pouch. Not a lot is known about the young tree kangaroo's first attempts at tree-climbing. It has a long tail like its mother's, but neither of them use their tails to hang on to the branches. They are merely aids to balance. Climbing is done only with the help of their clawed feet. The forelegs are longer and more powerful than those of the ground kangaroo. At the moment, this baby is staying cosily in its mother's pouch. From that position of safety, it can look out on the world and take a lively interest in everything its mother does throughout the day.

▶ The common raccoon is found widely throughout the United States of America, though more commonly in the south. A litter of up to six cubs is born in a tree nest. They are very small and remain in the nest for seven weeks. They stay with the mother for a whole year, learning to hunt for frogs, worms and insects, and to steal the eggs from birds' nests.

▼ The De Brazza guenon of Africa, unlike other guenons, lives in a family group rather than a troop. This baby spent several weeks clinging upside down to its mother's tummy. Now, though still very small, it can get about on its own and is already beginning to sprout the beard that is characteristic of the fully-grown monkey of this species.

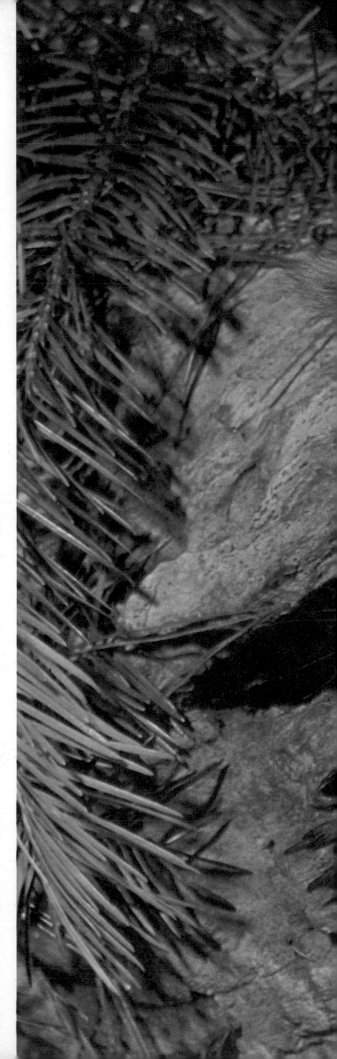

Antelopes belong to a large family of animals which also includes sheep, goats and oxen. As a whole, members of the family are known as bovids. Antelopes are found in all the continents of the world, but there are none in Australia. All the males have hollow, unbranched horns, but not all females. None of them sheds its horns. Fully-grown antelopes vary in size according to the species. Some of them are as big as cows. Others are no bigger than rabbits. This tiny baby suni will grow to no more than 30 centimetres (12 inches) high at the shoulder. Sunis are among the smallest of the antelope. They come from the open scrublands of east and central Africa. The baby is able to struggle to its feet almost as soon as it is born. Like all antelope, sunis depend on hearing, scent and fleetness of foot for protection.

Australia has several species of marsupial mice like this fat-tailed dunnart mother with her young. The babies are nursed in her backward-facing pouch until they grow too big for it. Then they all cling on desperately to their mother's back wherever they can get a hold and hitch a ride. The babies will grow to be about 9 centimetres (3½ inches) long in the body with a similar length of tail. When they can fend for themselves, they eat mainly insects.

Monkey mothers nurse their babies very much as human mothers do. This baby vervet monkey was cradled in its mother's arms while she fed it. On the move, it clung to the fur of her tummy and twined its tail with hers. Vervets live in troops of up to fifty and spend much of their time on the ground.

Geckos are one of the families of lizards. There are about four hundred different species throughout the world. This one, the gonatodes, has just hatched from its egg on the island of Trinidad in the West Indies. From the start, the baby will fend for itself. Geckos have tiny hairlike filiaments on the underside of their 'fingers'. These enable them to climb up surfaces as smooth as glass.

This woodmouse mother is seen suckling her babies in their underground nest. When they are old enough, they will leave the nest and begin to feed on buds and seeds, including nuts the mother has stored for them near the nest. Woodmice are expert at opening nuts with their sharp front teeth which never wear down because they grow continuously. The babies soon learn to climb trees in their search for food.

This baby spotted cuscus is enjoying a juicy feed from half an orange provided by the photographer. The spotted cuscus is found in New Guinea and the north-eastern tip of Australia. Like many tree-dwelling animals, it has eyes set looking forwards to judge distances when leaping from branch to branch. It would seem that cuscuses breed all the year round, as the females rarely have an empty pouch.

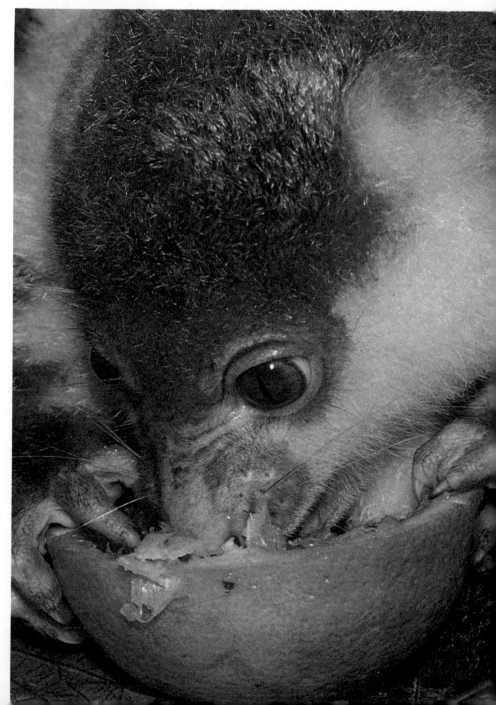

There are about 20,000 species of spiders. This wolf spider, from Arizona in the USA, carries her babies on her back. The female wolf spider is very much bigger than the male. When they have mated, she lays her eggs and attaches them by silk threads to her spinneret. The hatched out spiderlings are attached to her in the same way.

Some spiders use their silk-spinning skills to protect their eggs. This picture was taken on the island of Trinidad in the West Indies. It shows an egg cocoon of a member of the tenida family of spiders. The eggs are hatched out in this silky envelope. Then the baby spiderlings, seen in the photograph, emerge into the outside world.

Spiders usually have mouth parts with poison fangs with which they paralyse their prey. Some spiders are dangerous to humans. The black widow spider of North America can cause illness or even death with its bite. These black widow spiderlings move about the weblike threads of silk to which the eggs were attached. They will grow to about 1.2 centimetres (½ inch) long with black bodies and a red hourglass figure on the underside.

◀ The slow loris, a primate like monkeys and human beings, belongs to a family which includes the bush-babies. Its slow movements allow it to creep up on the birds it eats. The mother has one baby at any time of the year. It is born with fuzzy hair and quite alert.

▶ Scorpions, like the spiders on the previous pages, are arachnids. They are found in tropical and semi-tropical regions and even among snow-covered mountains. This spinigerus mother and her young were photographed in the Arizona desert of the USA. When the mother is foraging at night, she carries her babies on her back. Days are spent in their lair.

▶ Kangaroos are the best-known of the Australian marsupials. The great kangaroo can reach a length of 2.5 metres (8 feet), yet the new-born baby can nestle in a teaspoon. As soon as it is born, naked and almost helpless, it crawls into the mother's pouch where it feeds from her teats. It grows rapidly, but seems reluctant to leave the pouch, often hanging half out of it.

There are more than 300 species of hummingbird, all of them from the American continents, mostly from the south. They include the smallest bird in the world, the bee hummingbird which is only 5 centimetres (2 inches) from the tip of its beak to the end of its tail. The largest hummingbird is four times as long. This fledgling *Archilochus alexandri,* as soon as it has learned to fly, will be able to flap its wings so fast that it will hover in one spot in the air. Like all hummingbirds, its wings move in shoulder sockets, making this rapid flapping possible.

Marine turtles spend most of the time in water but the females come ashore to lay their eggs. Four or five clutches are buried separately above the tideline, around 100 eggs in each. Two or three months later, the hatched babies dig themselves out of the sand and scuttle down to the water.

The male praying mantis puts on a courting display for the much larger female in order to reduce her feeding urge. It rarely works. The female usually eats the male after mating. These young praying mantises soon learn to snatch smaller insects with the sharp spikes sticking out of their powerful forelegs.

BIG BABIES

Big animals have their own particular problems with their babies. Nature has found many different ways to help the mother of a big baby. Some are more successful than others. Long-legged and tall babies are born almost ready to stand on their own feet so that they can follow their mothers in search of food or to run away from enemies.

Heavy babies usually have strong mothers to look after them. The hippopotamus mother takes her baby to the water as soon as possible. She teaches it to swim by letting it ride on her back for a while. In the water, they are buoyed up so that they can both take the weight off their feet.

Some babies are particularly small in relation to their parents' size, and these will grow quickly. Growing babies need plenty of food. The mother is usually well-supplied with milk or she weans her young early, like the tigress feeding her cubs meat at six weeks.

► This young zebra foal was up on its feet soon after its birth. It must be ready from its earliest days to follow its mother in search of water and grazing, and to run away from an enemy when the herd takes to its heels.

This pair of young tawny owls have grown tired of waiting in the nest for their parents to bring them their breakfast. They have found a look-out post on a nearby branch. Already, they have the soft, downy body feathers of all owls. Soon, their wings will grow with furry flight feathers. This plumage is designed to reduce noise when they hunt for themselves, swooping by night on mice, voles, frogs or even fish.

Storks are birds that need an outsize nest for the growing brood. In Holland and Germany, it is thought to be lucky if a pair of storks nest on your rooftop. People build special platforms to tempt the birds to choose their houses. Storks make sure their babies' food is well chewed before they swallow it. They chew it themselves before they give it to them. Perhaps the care they take gave rise to the legend that storks bring human babies.

Most animal mothers reject their older youngsters as soon as new babies are born. Not so elephants. They pay as much attention to those almost fully grown as they do to the smallest babe. Elephants are sometimes not weaned until they are eight or nine years old. The older ones have no jealousy of the babies. In fact, they will help their mother to look after their younger brothers and sisters. This Asiatic elephant baby might even drink milk from another baby elephant's mother who is not its own.

This North American black bear cub is full of curiosity. It is forever wandering off on little foraging expeditions of its own. In this way, it learns about the world around it, ready for the day when it will have to hunt for its own food. For its first two years, the mother will make sure it never wanders too far away from her. Almost as soon as it can walk, the black bear cub learns to climb trees. If danger threatens, the mother chases all her cubs up a tree to wait there in safety until she has dealt with the danger or until it passes.

A female elephant retires into a thicket, with one or two other females to protect her, while she has her baby. The calf, as it is called, weighs 91 kilogrammes (200 pounds), as much as a full-grown man, and stands almost 1 metre (3.28 feet) high. Within an hour, it has learned to walk and very soon will be up to all sorts of playful antics like this calf.

Young animals often fight among themselves, though usually without malice. These two brown bear cubs will not use their teeth or claws on each other. Their battle is a friendly bout, just for practice. They are learning to use their developing muscles for the day when they might have to fight in earnest, against an enemy or to establish leadership.

This baby chacma baboon clung to the fur of its mother's tummy for the first five weeks of its life. Then it began riding on her back where it could get a better view of the world. Chacma baboons live in southern Africa in troops of about thirty, though as many as 200 have been seen together. The males are always ready to defend the females while they rear their young.

This young chimpanzee will stay with its mother until it is about six years old. That is the age when young males join the adult males in the community. Females tend to stay loosely together, though friendships develop between brothers and sisters who will groom each other. This youngster was photographed in Kahuzi Biega National Park, Zaire, in Central Africa.

These two young giant pandas are among the world's rare animals. They will grow to a length of about 1.5 metres (5 feet). They have an extra pad on their forepaws, a sixth 'finger' for gripping the bamboo shoots they like to chew. They also eat birds and small mammals. They are solitary animals, and not a lot is known about the life of the baby in the wild. They are related to the raccoon (page 46).

Most cats are solitary animals, but these playful cubs are members of a group called a pride. Their lioness mother left the pride to give birth to them in a secluded spot. The babies weigh about 1.5 kilogrammes (over 3 pounds). This pair of lion cubs have survived the times when the mother left them alone while she went hunting. About half the cubs born in the wild fall victim to predators.

Eagle owls take little trouble with their nests, built among rocks above a river or in the hollow of a tree. They simply choose a shallow depression and line it with leaves. The eggs hatch at intervals, those chicks that emerge last often being smaller than the others. Then they are in danger from their own brothers and sisters who often eat them. This is Nature's way of making sure that only the strong and fit survive into adult life. This chick is big and bold enough to leave the nest and explore its surroundings. In a few months, it will grow into one of the largest of owls.

◀ There are a number of wild relatives of the domestic cattle specially bred for dairy produce and meat. One of them is the African buffalo. This buffalo cow gave birth to her calf at the end of the rainy season when the grazing is at its best. Within ten minutes of birth, the calf struggled to its feet. For its first few days, it spent most of its time sleeping while its mother was grazing. The buffalo is one of the fiercest of all animals. This mother will even fight off an attack from a lion to protect her calf. Those horns are formidable weapons.

▲ The golden eagle is one of the largest and most magnificent birds of prey. It lives in the mountains of North America and Europe, swooping down over the valleys in search of small mammals to eat. It was chosen by the leaders of the ancient Roman Empire as a symbol of strength and reproduced on their battle standards. Its nest is an untidy collection of sticks and leaves on a high rocky ledge. This young chick is as scruffy as its home and will take about four years to grow the splendid plumage of its parents. Yet already it has that aggressive look.

The jaguar is a native of South America and the south-western states of the USA. There, the female makes a rough nest among the undergrowth or in a patch of flattened grass to give birth to her cubs. This one will grow to weigh well over 100 kilogrammes (220 pounds) and reach a length of 2.5 metres (8 feet). The mother breeds at intervals of only two or three years. Kittens mature at two years.

This is a North American puma, sometimes called the cougar or mountain lion. For the first two years of its life, it will hunt with its mother, in the daytime up in the mountains above the timberline, at night if they venture down on to the prairie. They will often store a kill in the snow to keep it refrigerated.

▲ Sheep and goats were the first wild animals to be herded by early man in the New Stone Age more than 10,000 years ago. This wild mountain kid may have a mixture of domesticated varieties in its forebears. The baby mountain goat has the urge to climb from its earliest days, practising even on its mother's back.

▶ The roe deer of Europe and Asia is a family animal, one buck and two or three females moving about together. Kids, usually born as twins, stay in hiding while the mother is grazing. She returns to them two or three times a day to suckle them. At two weeks old, the kids are ready to follow the doe.

This ostrich hatched from a clutch of six to eight eggs, each weighing about 1.36 kilogrammes (3 pounds), the largest eggs of any bird. Male and female take turns to sit on the eggs for forty days. The newly emerged chick is already 30 centimetres (12 inches) tall. Males will grow to 2.1 metres (7 feet). As soon as the chick has dried out, it can run. Fully grown in eighteen months, it will reach speeds of 64 kilometres per hour (40 miles per hour). Ostriches sleep for only fifteen minutes at a time, and their great height gives them a good view across the grasslands where they live. Grazing herds of zebras and antelopes use these timid birds as an early warning system of approaching danger.

At a week old, this giraffe calf began to nibble grass, though it will not be weaned completely from its mother's milk until it is nine months old. Yet some baby giraffes are known to spend weeks away from their mothers, so the milk cannot be an essential part of their diet. Half the calves die in their first year which may be due to lack of motherly care.

This giraffe calf was carried for sixteen months before it was born. Its birth involved a drop of about 2.5 metres (8 feet) to the ground. The baby has a lot of falling to do before it manages to stand upright. If it is a male, it will grow to 5.5 metres (18 feet). The female is 1 metre (3.28 feet) shorter.

▲ Orang-utan means 'man of the woods' in the Malay language. Orang-utans are apes living in the tropical forests of Sumatra and Borneo. The females have one baby at a time and suckle it for seven months, cradling it in their long arms everywhere they go. Then the baby learns to walk along the branches of trees, gripping on to the hair on its mother's rump.

▶ Baboons are monkeys living in the open grasslands of East Africa. When a large troop is on the move, the mothers and babies walk in the middle with the mature males, while younger males provide a protective screen around them. The baby, born black, clings to its mother's breast, though others are allowed to hold and groom it. When a baby squeals, adults rush to its aid.

A mother polar bear digs a cave in an Arctic snowdrift to give birth to her cubs. The cubs are between 18 and 30 centimetres (7–12 inches) long and weigh about 0.7 kilogrammes (1½ pounds) at birth. The mother stays with them in the cave for up to 140 days, suckling them and losing up to half her body weight in the process. The cubs fend for themselves after the second summer.

There are a number of races of brown bears, including the European, the blue, the Syrian and the grizzly. This grizzly bear cub, who seems to have temporarily mislaid its mother, lives in the coniferous forests of the north-western USA. It was born in a den, a natural cave or sheltered spot. At birth, it weighed only about 340 grammes (12 ounces), but it can grow to weigh 453 kilogrammes (1000 pounds). Adult male grizzlies are so strong, they can carry away a 400-kilogramme (900-pound) bison. This cuddly cub will grow into a wandering giant, peaceful enough except when it is cornered or needs to defend its young. If that happens, there is no fighter to be more dreaded than a grizzly.

▼ This youngster is the kind of antelope called an impala and is one of the more common antelopes. Its mother left the herd in December to give birth to her lamb, as it is called, on her own. December is the end of the wet season in Rhodesia where this lamb was born. At that time there is plenty of new, juicy grass for the nursing mother and for the lamb's first nibbles. By February, this male lamb was already beginning to sprout horns.

More than a third of Africa is open grassland, called savannah, home of this cheetah cub. Born in a litter of three to five, on average half the cheetah's young fail to survive their first six months. Cheetahs hunt small antelopes in pairs or family parties. When it grows up, this cub will be able to run at 112 kilometres per hour (70 miles per hour).

The rhinoceros is one of the heavyweights of the animal world, second only to the elephant in size and power. A new-born baby, at 55 centimetres (20 inches) high, is small compared with its mother, but already perfectly formed. The baby is born with no horns, but the stumps start to appear in a few weeks. Within a week or two, still suckling, the baby begins to graze.

▲ The mother hippopotamus leaves the herd to find a bed of reeds which she tramples down to form a nest. There, her baby is born and is active within a few hours. When it is a few weeks old, the baby is taken to the water where it joins the herd with its mother. They spend all day in water, coming out at night to feed. This baby may reach a weight of 3 tonnes (nearly 3 tons). Other females will help to look after it when the mother is feeding.

◄ This baby white rhinoceros is only three days old. There are five species of rhinoceros and the white from Africa is the biggest, weighing up to 3.55 tonnes (3½ tons). The other African species is the black rhinoceros. They both have two horns, as does the rare Sumatran rhino. The Javan, also very rare, and the Indian have single horns and folds of thick hide that make them look as if they are in armour.

This playful, kittenish baby will grow to be a ruthless hunter. It is a puma cub. Its kind are found in North and South America. The mother brings up her young to be tough. They are born in a rock cavern, perhaps, with no bedding to lie on. This cub will lose its spotted coat as it grows, becoming an all-over, darker brown. The mountain puma is much larger than its cousin that hunts the prairies where a shortage of game is reducing its numbers.

A tiger cub may be born on its own or one of a litter of up to five. It is suckled by its mother for the first six weeks, and then she gives it meat. By then, the cubs are already following their mother on the hunt though they take no part until they are six months old. Even then, the mother brings down the prey, allowing her cubs to kill it. Tigers are the biggest cats, males averaging 180 kilogrammes (400 pounds) and 2.75 metres (9 feet) long.

WATER BABIES

Water is essential to living things. The story of life began in the salt and fresh waters of the world. When plants and then animals left that watery world to live on the land, they still had need of water. Some animals have gone back to live with it, at least in part.

Most of them returned to the waters in their search for food. Many seabirds and water fowl became expert at catching fish, others feed on the weeds and insects found in or near water. Some animals, like the water vole, feed entirely on land, but take to the water to escape their enemies. Some, like frogs, spend most of their lives on land but have young that grow up in water. Others, like seals, spend most of their lives in water but return to the land to give birth to and rear their babies.

Every animal has its own ways with water. Here is how some baby animals learn to live with it from an early age.

◄ These newly-hatched goslings are ready to leave the nest and take to the water almost at once. They will follow their parents for comfort and protection but fend for themselves in the never-ending battle for food.

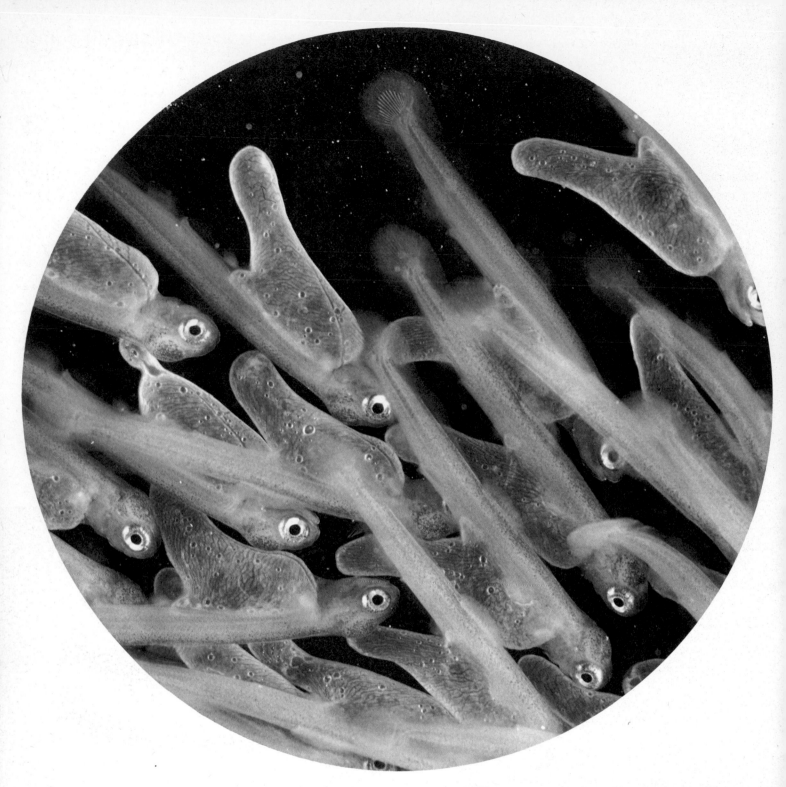

▲ A female salmon lays her eggs in a hollow in the bed of a stream and covers them with gravel. These hatched babies with yolk sacks to feed them are called 'alevins'. When the yolk sacks are gone, they will feed on insect larvae. After a year, called 'parr', they head for the sea. A year or more later, they return to the river headwaters to breed. Those that return after only one winter in the sea are known as 'grilse'.

▶ There are several species of sticklebacks. Most can live in fresh or salt water. This newly-hatched three-spine stickleback may have begun life in a quiet corner of a stream or in a pool above the tideline of the sea-shore where the father built his nest to attract the mother to lay her eggs in it. The father will then have entered the nest to fertilise the eggs and remained on guard until they hatched.

Here are three fertilised eggs of the three-spine stickleback, greatly enlarged, showing the baby fish developing inside them. The female has long ago left the nest. Only the male remains on guard, fighting off other creatures, even of his own kind, who may try to rob the nest. During this period, the careful father changes to a brighter blue colour with a red patch on the front part of his belly, earning him the name of Red Throat. The babies that hatch from these eggs may grow to between 5 and 10 centimetres (2 to 4 inches).

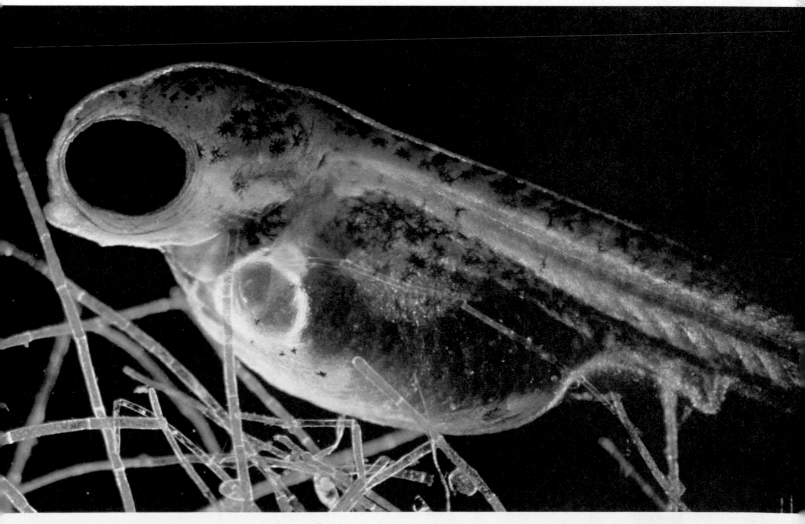

This fluffy chick looks as though it is practising for a career as a clown. Yet it will grow into one of the largest and most graceful of seabirds. It is a black-browed albatross, one of many species of albatrosses that nest in clifftop colonies on remote oceanic islands. Its parents perform elaborate courtship displays, even though they have been together for several years. By late summer, this chick will be flying.

Swans, admired for their grace and beauty, have long been thought of as symbols of purity and goodness. A black swan, unknown in the northern hemisphere until recently, was imagined as evil, the opposite of the white swan. This family of black-necked swans lives in South America. They might be thought to be a cross between a northern white swan and the Australian black swan, but they are a separate species. Like all swans, they rear their cygnets with care.

Cats are usually supposed to dislike water. Yet the van cat of Turkey, the ocelot and the jaguar all take readily to water. This North American bobcat, the equivalent of the Eurasian and African wild cat, though still a kitten, is an able swimmer. It likes to keep its tail dry, though, by holding it aloft, clear of the water. It is a species of lynx and is equally at home in the forest or the desert. It will grow to a length of about 75 centimetres (30 inches) and become a swift and deadly hunter of rabbits and hares.

Crocodiles and alligators are among the few reptiles to care for their young after they have hatched. The parents of this American alligator build a mound with mud and vegetation in which the female lays her eggs. Heat is generated in the mound and this helps to incubate the eggs. The nest, like this one, is close to water, so that the babies can follow their parents in their first swimming lessons. All alligators and crocodiles have raised nostrils so that they can breathe while the rest of the body is submerged in the water. They can feed underwater, too, because of an air passage from the nostrils to the throat which has a valve to keep water out of the windpipe. They are fast swimmers, propelled by their powerful tails. Even on land, they can move faster than is generally supposed.

Sharks and rays are different from 'true' fish. They do not have the bony skeleton, but one made of cartilage or gristle which hardens only with age. They also have no swim-bladder to keep them afloat. They have to swim all the time to avoid sinking to the bottom of the sea. This does not matter so much for this torpedo ray mother who feeds on the creatures of the sea-bed. She has just given birth to her live young, tiny replicas of herself. She gives them no motherly care. They are ready to feed themselves. Torpedo rays have special cells that generate electricity to shock and paralyse their victims.

Sea lion babies need to spend a good deal of their early life resting on shore, until they become strong swimmers. These Galapagos sea lion pups have hauled themselves on to the black larva beach of an island in the group that gives them their name. One difference between a sea lion and a true seal is that the former has visible ears, unlike the tiny ear hole of the true seals. Sea lions are sometimes called 'eared' seals. They can also move their front flippers forward, making it easier for them to walk on land. In two to three months, the pups are weaned and sea-going.

This baby grey seal is one of the 'true' seals, as compared with the fur seals, sea lions and walruses. The grey seal is born with a white puppy coat like this one. At first, it is very thin, but the cow feeds it on a rich, fatty milk, and it puts on weight rapidly. After three weeks, the pup is weaned and sheds its puppy coat. Its short puppyhood is over. It must take to the sea, to search for its own food. Like all true seals, it uses its hind flippers for swimming. Other seals use their more mobile front flippers. The grey seal is one of a huge colony that comes ashore to breed. The common seal is more adapted to a continuous life at sea. Pups, born in sea-going coats, are swimming the same day.

◀ The Eurasian otter is a freshwater mammal. The young are hidden in a shallow burrow in a river bank, in hollow trees, in between rocks and among reed beds. They are taught to swim at eight weeks old and are very reluctant learners. Both parents feed the babies and later teach them to hunt.

▼ The smallest sea mammal is the sea otter, the males reaching 1.5 metres (5 feet) in length. They rarely leave the sea, even when mating and breeding. The female floats on her back to suckle her young. Sea otters do not have the layer of fat that keeps other sea mammals warm in the water. Instead, a warm jacket of air is trapped between the hairs of their thick fur.

Common frogs spend part of their lives in water and part on dry land. The female lays her eggs in water in a tight mass which swells up and floats on the surface. These tiny tadpoles, hatched out from the frogspawn, feed on the jelly until they have grown enough to swim about. Then they start to eat the greenery of water plants, until they have developed lungs and legs so that they can leave the water.

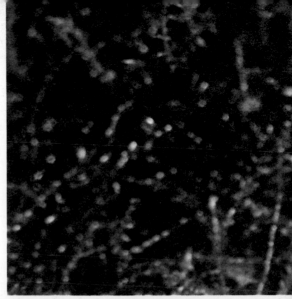

The midwife toad of western Europe has a strange method of parental care. The female lays her eggs on her hindlegs, from which the male removes them to wrap them around his own legs. After carrying them about for three weeks, he enters water where the tadpoles hatch.

▲ The sarus crane is a bird of the open grasslands of India. This chick's parents have paired for life, but each year they perform their courtship dance again. Both parents take their share of sitting on the eggs and feeding the young that hatch from them. This chick will grow rapidly bigger and more long-legged until it stands 1.8 metres (nearly 6 feet) tall. Despite its great wings, it will rarely fly far from water.

▶ This water spider has collected bubbles of air between its legs to form a large underwater bubble like a diving bell. Here it stores food and mates. Its eggs are wrapped in a silk cocoon and left in the diving bell to hatch out, when a store of food will be already waiting to feed the tiny spiderlings. The egg cocoon can be seen through the diving bell where the mother spider has just placed it.

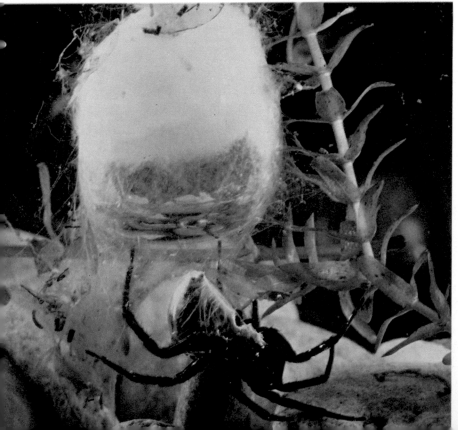

▲ Here is a troop of pochard ducklings in frenzied pursuit of their mother. The pochard population of Britain is increased every winter by foreign visitors. Pochards make a nest of rushes in the grass alongside a lake. six to twelve greenish or yellowish-white eggs are laid between April and June. The ducklings take to the water as soon as they have dried out, following their parents in the search for tasty waterweed, insects and small shellfish. The drakes have distinctive chestnut heads, black necks and breasts.

Beavers are still widespread in North America, though rarer now in Europe and Asia. They live in pairs or family groups, storing food in lodges and building dams to keep the water level up around the lodge. Three or four young, called kittens, are born in April or May. The male moves out to a burrow on the lake shore while the young are being suckled. For two years or more, this kitten will stay with its parents, learning to fell trees and build dams. In the USA, beavers are dropped by parachute into mountain areas to build their dams and prevent soil erosion.

South American fur seal pups can be found on the southern shores of South America and the Falkland Islands. They are born in December, midsummer for those regions. Already, though not yet four months old, this pup may spend up to two weeks at a time at sea. Soon, it will shed its present coat and replace it with a thick brown underfur covered by an olive-grey overcoat. When another year has gone by, this coat will be replaced yet again by a silvery-grey one. Born about 75 centimetres (30 inches) long and weighing about 6.5 kilogrammes (14 pounds), the male pup will become three times the length and 32 times the weight.

This Eurasian water vole is sitting at its back door, eating a piece of apple. The front door of its burrow will be underwater. This baby, like an otter cub, will be terrified of the water at first. Forced into it, it will kick and scream until it is removed. The mother has to coax it in and to teach it to swim alongside her. In the end, it will grow into a strong swimmer. Water voles live in colonies and store food for the winter in their burrows, though they do not hibernate. They burrow about under the snow, with their thick coats, furry feet and hairy tails to keep them warm.

Gannets build their nests on the flat tops of small, off-shore islands. Most birds have a bare patch, where the feathers have moulted in the breeding season, so that the warmth of the parents' bodies can reach the eggs. Gannets do not have this 'brood patch'. Instead, they incubate their eggs between their webbed feet. They are poor parents, leaving their chicks to fend for themselves after about two months. Born naked, the chick soon develops a fluffy, creamy-white plumage like the one on the right. This grows into the smooth, black and white plumage of the older chick on the left while, at the same time, the baby's black beak changes into the yellow bill of the adult bird.

The black tern passes over south-east England in the spring and early summer on its way north to its nesting grounds. It builds a nest of sticks and floating vegetation, wedged between reeds and roots on the edge of inland waters. When the chicks are first hatched out, they have a brown and white, fluffy plumage. This changes to grey and white and remains that colour for the whole of the first year. Only in their second year do they develop the lovely, slatey-grey deepening to dark grey on the underparts. In the winter, these underparts and the neck turn white. Black terns are found across North America and the northern regions of Europe and Asia.

HIDDEN BABIES

An animal is at its most helpless stage when it is a baby. This is true of even the fiercest and fastest of creatures. Half the cubs born to lionesses fall victim to predators while their mothers have left them to go hunting. Fawns of the fallow deer are left alone, barely concealed, while the mother is grazing.

Some mothers leave their young to take their chances with only the protection Nature has provided, the cunning camouflage of some caterpillars, for instance. Other mothers go to a great deal of trouble to keep their babies hidden and to protect them even after they have left the nest or the burrow.

Since one animal's family is often another animal's food supply, Nature has arranged matters so that few creatures are completely protected throughout their babyhood and growing up period. This section shows how some babies are hidden from their natural enemies, with varying success, until they are ready to face life alone.

► Hedgehog babies are born in a nest of dry leaves well hidden in dense undergrowth. At three weeks, their sharp spines have hardened, deterring all but foxes and badgers.

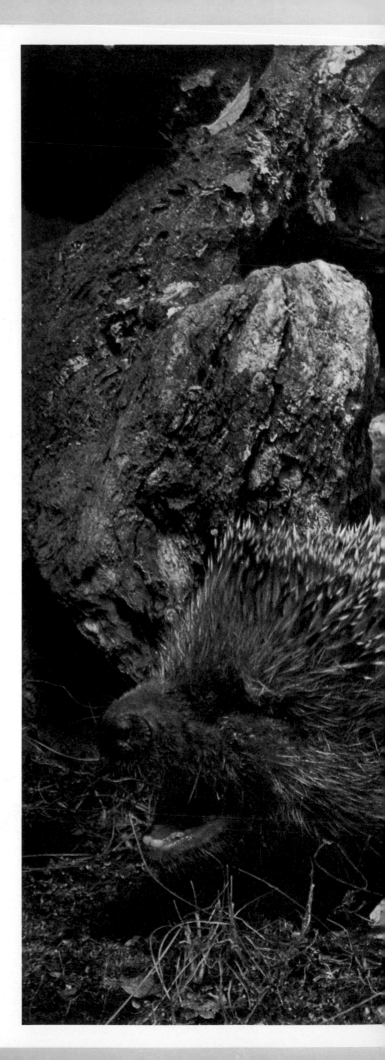

The female badger is a careful housewife and mother, keeping the nest burrow very clean and even using another burrow as a lavatory. The whole system of burrows, often shared by several families, is called the 'set'. This baby, at six weeks old already the size of an adult rabbit, will be ready to leave the set in a fortnight or so. Yet it is welcome to stay on through the autumn and winter, eating the solid food well chewed first by its mother. Badgers, cruelly hunted by men, have become very hidden and secretive animals.

These baby shrews were born blind, naked and wrinkled in a nest of hay or straw, often roofed in for added warmth and concealment. They will grow into the smallest of all mammals. Tiny mammals lose heat more quickly than bigger ones. Shrews must eat their own weight in food every day to keep alive. When the babies are old enough to leave the nest, they form a chain behind the mother, each hanging on to the tail in front. They hunt above ground and in other animals' tunnels, day and night.

The grass rat of southern Arabia and central Africa builds a nest of grass in an underground burrow where the litter of young is born. The tiny babies are blind at first, but already covered with long but rather sparse hair. This lively youngster is chewing a grass stem to exercise its jaws. It still lives entirely from its mother's milk, but is practising for the day when it must take to the almost entirely vegetarian diet of its kind. Before it is a month old, it may be joined by a second litter.

There comes a time in the life of even the shyest of baby animals when it must venture out of hiding and face the dangers of the outside world. With mammals, this period of the growing up process occurs when the baby is weaned. Either the mother no longer has the milk supply to go on suckling her young, or she decides it is time for them to learn to feed themselves. This young African bush squirrel has been lucky enough to find a coconut already opened, but it must learn to open smaller nuts for itself. Its first efforts may not be successful. By watching older squirrels and by trial and error, it learns to bite a small hole in the top of a nut, insert its front teeth, turn them and split the nut into two halves.

The pursuit of peaceful grazing animals like antelope by the big meat-eating animals like lions is a well-known drama of the animal world. Hidden among the tall grass, a lesser drama is taking place. Small meat-eaters, like the mongoose, are also stalking their prey. Here two youngsters emerge to begin following the mother on her hunting trips and to taste their first meal of snake or mouse.

Another of the hidden hunters is the stoat. It ranges throughout the coniferous forest regions of the northern hemisphere and even into the Arctic tundra. The female makes a nest in a hole, a hollow tree or under rocks. Her babies, born covered in soft, white fur, develop a black tip to their tails at three weeks. At five weeks old, as they begin to assume the brown upper colouring of their parents, they are weaned. Then, they are ready to join the adult, family hunting parties. As babies, they have been playful animals, developing their agility by twisting and turning together in endless games. Soon, they must face the harsh reality of the hunter's life. They will prey on rats, mice, rabbits, birds, insects and earth worms. In the winter snows, their coats will turn to pure white again with a black tip to the tail. Then, known as ermine, they are well enough camouflaged to creep up on their prey unseen.

The long-tailed tit is only 14 centimetres (5½ inches) long, and most of that is tail. A mating pair build a nest in the depths of a bush or a hedge. It is one of the masterpieces of the builder's art, made from moss, lichen, wool and spiders' webs, and lined with up to 2000 fluffy feathers. It forms an oval ball with an entrance hole on one side close to the top. Here, the female lays six to fifteen eggs, speckled with red. At night, about a dozen growing chicks and both parents squeeze into the stifling, feathery ball of the nest. Long-tailed tits are seen in groups of about half a dozen, chasing insects among the hedgerows and woods. Like all tits, they are extremely acrobatic on the branches.

The reed warbler is a summer visitor to Britain, found among the reed beds and marshes of southern England and as far north as Yorkshire. It is rare farther north or in Wales. Its nest is a carefully constructed deep cup, suspended between reeds, and made mainly of grass, moss and wool. Sometimes, it might be found in the drier situation of a bush. Four or five eggs are laid between May and July, greenish-white and blotched with olive. The parent's colouring is not at all conspicuous among the reeds, making it difficult to spot as it carries food to its chicks in the well-concealed nest. Bird-watchers identify it from the harsh chatter and surprisingly low notes coming from among the reeds.

Lemmings provide a main source of food for flesh-eaters like stoats, Arctic foxes and snowy owls. They are also poorly adapted to the cold in the northern regions they inhabit. For protection and to keep warm, they build networks of tunnels beneath the snow with nests where they can maintain a temperature of 10°C (50°F) when it is well below freezing point on the surface. The first babies of the year, born in June as soon as the snow melts, are weaned in fourteen days and able to breed themselves by August or September.

Jackals belong to the family of wild dogs which includes foxes. These silver-backed jackal pups look very much like fox cubs. They are just two of a litter of eight playing near the entrance to their den dug into an ant hill. As they grow, they will develop the long legs, slender bodies and lean jaws of the typical hunter. Different species of jackals range across southern Asia and Africa. The shrieking cry of a pack of jackals is even more bloodcurdling than that of hyenas. Their Arabic name, deeb, means 'howler'.

The goldfinch is one of the smaller and perhaps the most handsome of the European finches, now introduced into North America, Australia and New Zealand. Its nest is well concealed in small trees or bushes and made from grass, fine roots, moss, lichen, wool and thistledown. It is often prettily decorated with garlands of flowers. The females lay four to six white eggs speckled with brown and purple. The chicks are fed on insects and larvae, but soon begin eating seeds after they have left the nest. Flocks of goldfinch are called 'charms'.

The grasslands of North
America are the home of
the prairie dog, which is not a
dog at all but a ground squirrel.
One species, the black-tailed
prairie dog, digs underground
'towns' of hundreds of
burrows. The larger towns are
divided into wards with each
family group forming what is
called a 'coterie' of one male,
three females and about six
young. Burrow entrances, like
the one from which these two
youngsters are emerging, are
often walled against flooding.
When danger is spotted, a
dog-like bark of warning sends
everyone scuttling for cover.

The wood hoopoes of Africa, of which there are six species, differ from the common hoopoe that is a summer visitor to Britain. Wood hoopoes are slimmer and have no crest. They seldom leave the trees, whereas common hoopoes feed on the ground. All hoopoes are dirty housekeepers. This purple wood hoopoe has chosen a hole in a trunk for a nest. Nests are often not lined, and droppings and stale food never removed. The female has a scent gland at the base of the tail which adds to the stench during the brooding period. Wood hoopoes fly among the trees making grunting noises in the absence of a singing voice.

The red fox is not a good digger. It makes its own burrow or 'earth' only in soft, sandy soil. Otherwise, it uses a disused badger set or rabbit warren. A litter of four to six is born in March or April. The cubs are blind for their first two weeks, but after about a month they start emerging from the earth to play and practise fighting with each other. After they are weaned, the mother continues to feed them, first with food she has chewed for them and later with whole rats and mice. When the youngsters have been taught to hunt for themselves, they leave the parents who stay together, often helping each other with their hunting.

▼ The young of insects cannot rely on their small size to avoid the keen eyes of the animals, especially birds, that feed on them. This is the caterpillar of the bordered beauty moth. It has legs only at the front and rear. When it is not feeding, it clings to a twig by its rear legs and juts out the rest of its body at a rigid angle, imitating a branching twig. Its colour matches poplar or willow bark.

▲ Here is the bordered beauty moth that emerges from the chrysalis of the caterpillar in the picture on the left. The moth, too, has markings that help to break up its outline and merge with its surroundings for concealment. Moths, however, have to live only long enough to mate and lay eggs to ensure the survival of the species. The eggs of this moth are laid on the poplar or willow tree, the food plant of the caterpillar.

▶ There are about 2000 different species of leaf and stick insects, most of them living in tropical climates, though four or five of them are found in Europe. Their bodies, wings and legs resemble withered or growing twigs or are flattened into the shape of leaves. They remain quite still all day and move about to feed at night. Their eggs look like seeds. The picture shows *Clitumnus axtradentatus*, a stick insect from Asia, with several newly-hatched insects.

FARM BABIES

Man, the hunter, chased other animals, killed them and ate them. His struggle for survival was as simple as that. Man, the farmer, learned to corral his game, to keep it on the hoof, to kill it only when he needed fresh meat to supplement the corn he grew. As early man learned to harvest grain and select the best for replanting, so he learned to pick out the best beasts for breeding. The domestication of animals had begun. That was 10,000 years ago.

The wolf had already been lurking around the camp fires of the hunter for centuries. Cubs or wounded wolves were used as decoys to attract other game. Wolves joined in the chase, even learned to herd game towards the hunters' spears. Cubs kept as pets by children enjoyed living with people. As their diet and habits changed, they grew doglike.

Thus were animals trained to work for man and bred to supply his needs. Now, many of the world's animals depend on man for their entire existence.

▶ Sheep were probably the first animals to be herded and bred by man. Now, every year, the miracle of lambing takes place on farms all over the world.

This inquisitive pair of newly-hatched farmyard chicks have a long and complicated ancestry behind them. Modern free-range breeds of domestic fowl have names like Wyandotte, Rhode Island Red, Orpington and Plymouth Rock. Yet all were probably bred from one original species, the Indian jungle fowl. It was domesticated in India as far back as 3200 BC and found its way into Europe through Persia and Egypt. Once the hatched chicks have dried out, they can stand, peck for food and run around within the hour. The hen has little mothering to do.

This farmyard duckling belongs to a family of water birds which also includes geese and swans. Strictly speaking, the name 'duck' should apply only to the female, the male being called a drake. Domesticated ducks are descended from the wild duck or mallard which has become a popular water bird in parks and is common in the countryside. They are surface swimmers.

This is a baby wild sheep or mouflon, nowadays found mainly on the Mediterranean island of Sardinia. Even there, the wild sheep have interbred with domesticated breeds, so that the pure mouflon is quite rare. The various species of wild sheep have longer legs and bigger horns than domesticated breeds where the aim was to provide meat for food, wool for clothing and fat for candles.

▼ This is a young lamb of the blackface breed of domestic sheep, reared on mountainsides and moorland. Sheep were perhaps the first animals ever herded by mankind. Dogs helped man long ago with that job and despite the modern mechanisation of farming, they still help the shepherd nowadays.

▲ Cats have been farmyard animals ever since they were first domesticated by the early Egyptians thousands of years ago. They are all descended from the wild cat *Felis silvestris.* Wild cats are solitary animals, never hunting in packs like dogs. All the various breeds of domesticated cat have remained comparatively aloof from mankind, nor have we found as many jobs for them as we have for the dog. Nevertheless, for us as for the ancient Egyptians, they keep rats and mice away from the corn rick and farm buildings, as this farmyard family no doubt will do.

The almost naked, short-legged, fat and lumbering farmyard pig bears little resemblance to the fierce wild boar of the forest. Yet all domestic pigs have been bred from the wild woodland ancestor. The male wild boar is fast on its feet. It will charge an enemy fearlessly and rip open its body with the sharp, curving tusks growing from the lower jaw. Males hunt alone. Females forage with their young and other sows in groups called 'sounders', often numbering up to fifty. One thing the wild boar has in common with its peaceful descendants is that it will eat almost anything. Mainly a plant-eater, grubbing up roots with its snout and gobbling up fallen fruits and nuts, it will also attack and eat small animals or scoop up insects and earthworms. Breeding over the centuries has produced a much bigger pig with a shorter head and smaller teeth, and eyes set forward in the head rather than looking out sideways.

Family life for farmyard animals has changed considerably from that of their wild ancestors. Provided with food by the farmer, cock and hen no longer need to pay any attention to the needs of their chicks who can scratch a living from the moment they leave the egg.

Farmyard animals form a mixed society where natural enemies learn to accept each other happily. Cats may be natural hunters, but this well-fed kitten has no reason to attack the hen who would be well able to defend herself if it did. The kitten learns to chase only those animals, like rats and mice, that run away. Those with a right to be there soon teach it the facts of farmyard life. Nowadays, the tendency is to keep animals separate, as in the batteries of the chicken farmer.

Ancient man domesticated animals not only for food but also to work for him. The wild asses of Africa and Asia were loaded with his baggage and harnessed to his ploughs and vehicles. The donkey has been bred over thousands of years from the African wild ass. Its remarkable strength for its size has made it a useful bearer of burdens and puller of carts. Its docile nature when treated with kindness has made it the favourite mount for small children.

Mankind hardly needed to tame the dog. Wolves crept close to his camp fires to beg or steal scraps of food. Orphan cubs made friendly pets for his children. From the North American, the Chinese, the Indian and the European wolf all the breeds of dogs known today have descended. Of all the wild animals, dogs have adapted best to the ways of man. This Old English sheepdog pup sitting with its mother is quite willing to join us as fellow worker or household pet to earn its living.

The wild animals most suited to domestication have been those that move in groups or herds. Having accepted a herd leader, they will be all the more ready to accept man as a leader. Slow-moving, browsing cattle were 'easy meat' for the early hunter. Their milk supply became an added food. Jersey cows and calves are bred for the quantity and richness of their milk. They have the short, sleek coat of cattle found in the lush, lowland meadows of mild climates.

Modern cattle have descended from two wild species: the Eurasian auroch and the zebu or hump-backed ox of Africa and southern Asia. When man had taken over leadership of the herd, he began to learn how to interbreed cattle to produce the many varieties that inhabit the ranches of stockbreeders throughout the world. Scottish Highland cows are bred for beef. Highland cattle have the shaggy coats of animals from colder, mountain regions. So breeding has adapted each to its own environment and to the needs of the farmer.

▶ Man managed to capture and tame the wild horse about 5000 years ago. A faster and more independent animal than the wandering cattle, it was soon to prove its usefulness as a beast of burden. There is now only one species of wild horse in the world. Called Przewalski's horse, it inhabits a few isolated parts of Mongolia. This New Forest pony may have been born in the 'wilds' of southern England, but its forebears once escaped from man's service.

▼ This foal, on the other hand, was born on a stud farm and will be trained to serve a human master. The days when horses provided the main motive power for transport or carried a fighting man into battle are, for them, happily over.

▶ This American palomino foal has been bred specially for its beautiful golden coat and blonde mane and tail. The horse was introduced into America by Europeans in the 16th century. Horses played a great role in the settlement of the pan-American continent. They have earned the honoured place they hold in the affairs of modern man.

HAPPY FAMILIES

There are many ways in which families behave in the animal kingdom, some of them strange and, perhaps, cruel to us. They all follow the same principal — the survival of the species.

Each baby animal is adapted to its environment as it grows up. At its birth it might need warmth or protection. Always, one or other, or both, of the parents is able and willing to provide the baby's immediate needs. Yet the law of life insists that the youngster should be able to fend for itself as soon as possible.

Sometimes, a young animal needs to learn a lot before it can cope with life on its own. Then the parents stay with it, providing its education by example. Sometimes, a young animal is able to fend for itself almost at once. It is not cruel, in that case, for the parents to leave it to get on with it.

Some individuals succeed, to live a long and full life. Others succumb to their enemies almost before their life has begun. It rests with Nature.

◀ The chimpanzee is as patient as any mother with her mischievous offspring. The affection of their family life is a delight to watch.

This is a family of meerkats, also called suricates, a species of mongoose living in the dry, open grasslands of southern Africa. The father helps to groom the babies, but their feeding, even after weaning, is left entirely to the mother. Families live a neighbourly life in large colonies and dig burrows in sandy banks where they sleep at night. Nests are made at the ends of longer burrows where the babies are nursed. Meerkats will attack enemies bigger than themselves.

Ostriches live in families of one cock and usually three hens and their young. The hens share a nest, each laying six to eight eggs—as many as twenty-four in one nest. Each egg is 15 centimetres (6 inches) long and weighs 1.36 kilogrammes (3 pounds)—the biggest eggs of any living bird, yet the smallest in relation to the bird that lays them. The hens shade them from the sun with outstretched wings during the day, and the cock stands guard at night. The first eggs to be laid are rolled out of the nest so that they incubate more slowly. In this way, all the chicks hatch at the same time. Then the whole family can move on together.

Despite her dependence on human beings, a pet bitch is a capable mother. She will make her own suitable arrangements for the confinement. Pups are often born in the strangest places. While she is suckling her young, the bitch can resent human interference. She likes to keep them clean and in order. If they wander too far, she will bring them back by force, and chastise them if she thinks they need it. If her chosen lair proves inconvenient or danger threatens, she will carry her pups one by one to a better or safer place. This Dandie Dinmont family are a breed of terrier.

▲ This family of fur seals could belong to a breeding colony that may number hundreds of thousands. The large male in the picture has two wives, one already with a baby. The mother suckles her young for three months. During this time, she has to return to the ocean to feed. The pup stays behind, at first lying with its flippers wrapped round itself to keep warm, but later becoming more adventurous. Between feeds, pups lose weight. During two-day feeding sessions, they may add as much as a third to their weight.

▶ The female walrus, like the fur seal, gives birth almost a year after mating. The calf is 1.25 metres (4 feet) long and weighs about 45 kilogrammes (100 pounds) at birth. It is born on the ice and needs its mother's protection to avoid freezing to death during the first three weeks of its life. The calf's tusks grow to about 2.5 centimetres (1 inch) in the first year, but can reach more than 1 metre (3.28 feet) in mature males.

The horse was introduced into the Middle East about 1800 BC when it was used to draw a fast chariot with the first spoked wheels. Since then, the horse has taken part in many of the wars men have fought with each other. By 1200 BC, armies had their troops of cavalry as well as chariotry. Horses became very important, bred for speed and endurance. The Arab horse is now the world's oldest and purest breed. The descendants of those battle-horses of long ago can be seen on every race-course. This Arab mare and her slender foal live happily together on a stud ranch near Phoenix in Arizona, USA. The youngster may yet become a racing champion.

Here is a gathering of quarter horses on an American stud farm. Originally a cross between 17th century Spanish and English horses, the quarter horse got its name from the quarter-mile races popular then, often along the main streets of the Western towns. The breed is now used for rodeo events.

This golden palomino mare in America has given birth to a chestnut foal. Known as the Golden Horse of the West, the palomino is not a true breed but a colour variety. Even when two thoroughbred palominos with the perfect colouring are mated, a palomino foal does not always result. Like all American horses, the palomino originates from Europe. Queen Isabella of Spain, who backed Columbus on his voyage of discovery, is known to have encouraged the breeding of palominos. They may have descended from Arabs. They are mentioned in ancient chronicles of the Kings of Yemen in southern Arabia. They are excellent saddle horses, popular for pleasure riding and in the show ring. Perhaps this foal will produce its own palomino offspring.

▲ This leopard cat mother, a native of East Asia, carries her kitten to a safe place. At five weeks old, leopard kittens look very much like domestic kittens. As they grow, their coats will change to white splashed with black. Father and mother meet only during the breeding season, and the male plays no part in the rearing of the young who also grow up to be solitary hunters.

▶ Most members of the cat tribe are solitary animals. Lions live the family or group life of the pride. A pride is not strictly a family since more than one adult male may be present. Usually, the lionesses in a pride are related. A typical pride might consist of two adult males, an aging female, two young females and cubs. The purpose of the pride seems to be the protection of the cubs. For its first weeks, however, the cub does not enjoy this protection. The lioness leaves the pride to give birth in a place of concealment some distance away. She has to leave her cubs while she is hunting for her own food. During these periods, the cubs are in great danger from predators.

Coots belong to the group of water birds that can swim underwater in the search for food, as compared with dabblers who are surface swimmers and can only dip their heads under to reach the tops of weeds. Coots are found in Europe, Asia and Australia. The nests are built of reeds on the verges of lakes and rivers, hidden among the vegetation. The chicks are fed by the father who will feed any chicks not too small or too large to be his own. Only when the chicks are about a fortnight old do their parents recognise them. Here, a mother coot has at last recognised her own brood of six youngsters. Now, both parents will protect them while they dabble and dive to feed themselves. Coots have feet with long, lobed claws well adapted to aid the agile swimmer.

Penguins have lived in the Antarctic oceans for 50 million years. Their ancestors arrived there when the climate was warmer to feed on the vast numbers of fish. In the absence of enemies on the remote islands, they lost the power of flight. Their wings shortened and evolved into flippers. Penguins became more at home in the sea, their small, dense feathers forming a protective covering like the scales of fish. They come ashore to mate and lay their eggs in pebble nests. Parents take turns to warm the chicks or catch fish for them.

▲ Family care among elephants extends to the whole herd. A mother may often suckle other calves than her own. Quarrels do occur between bulls when they compete for a cow, but they are soon settled by the superior strength of one of them. Calves are born weighing about 115 kilogrammes (250 pounds) and go on growing for the rest of their lives. A big bull can weigh 6.6 tonnes (6½ tons) at the age of forty. Such animals need to lose excess heat. They like nothing better than wallowing in water and plastering each other in mud. These African elephants cool the blood flowing through their big ears by flapping them.

▶ This gentoo penguin with its chicks belongs to one of the most southerly of all the species of penguin. Though, like all penguins, spending most of its time in the water, it comes ashore to breed. One of the sociable penguins, it forms colonies varying from a few pairs to millions of individuals. Competing for nesting space, they can be very quarrelsome and noisy. The nest is usually raised on a heap of stones to avoid it flooding when the snows melt. Normally, two eggs are laid. They are sometimes taken by raiding skuas, but there is time for another pair to be laid within the same season.

Waterbuck belong to the family of seventy-two species of African antelope. They are related to cattle and are cud-chewing, grazing animals. They keep close to water, retiring at night into the woodlands alongside rivers. This baby was born in woodland and left there alone during the day while the mother was grazing. Now it is old enough to leave the wood and follow its mother into the adjoining grasslands to graze. The females remain in small groups, joining up into herds of about thirty for protection while feeding.

This pair of caspian terns has brought a rather outsize meal of fish for their newly-hatched chick. These are the largest of the terns and breed almost everywhere except South America. They share their nesting sites with other species of terns in vast colonies, often covering the surface of whole islands.

This family of field voles has found a convenient rock under which to conceal the nest. Field vole nests are made of grass and often indistinguishable from the grass surrounding them, especially when a domed roof is added. These youngsters, two to three weeks old, are being weaned with their first solid food. At only six weeks old they will be mature enough to breed themselves. A female field vole may have as many as a dozen litters in a year. Such numerous creatures naturally come to form the staple diet of bigger mammals and birds, so that very few of them survive their first year, though always enough to maintain the species.

This American robin, like its European cousin, is one of the first birds in the spring to lay its eggs. The female is the nest-builder, making it from soft grass and lining it with mud. The male will do only a little light fetching and carrying for her. Again, it is the female who sits on the eggs, though the male will lend the odd beakful to help feed the chicks. The wide-open beak of the chick, lined in the case of the American robin with yellow, is a kind of signal. It arouses in the parent an irresistible urge to drop food into it. The baby beak opens at the merest sound or sight of the parent.

▲ The polar bear nursery has a 60—90 centimetre (2—3 foot) entrance tunnel, opening out into an oval 1.2 metres (4 foot) high chamber. It is built into the accumulation of snow against the side of a mountain. One or two, sometimes three babies, are born very small and sparsely covered in hair. They can hear at a month old and see a week later. They start to walk at seven weeks and are weaned at three months.

◄ This kodiak mother bear and her cub are a variety of the North American grizzly. The kodiak parents mate in midsummer, but the babies are not born until January or February. By then, the mother has retired into a cave or similar den for her winter sleep. The birth is easy with tiny babies. Their arrival disturbs her so little, she wakes just enough to suckle them.

▲ Ape and monkey mothers behave very much like human mothers with their babies. Here, a pair of baby leaf monkeys from the Holy Monkey Forest on the island of Bali in the East Indies, are cradled in their parents' arms. The babies have the grip of human babies, though they develop it sooner. Within a few hours of birth, a baby leaf monkey can cling so tightly to the fur of its mother's tummy that she can leap among the trees with it safely.

▶ The orang-utan is an ape, second in size only to the gorilla. Again, mother and baby look very human in their attitude if not their looks. Again, almost from birth, the baby can cling so tightly to its mother that it is perfectly safe as she swings about the trees, deep in the forests of Borneo or Sumatra. The baby is fed on the mother's milk with leaves and fruit chewed by her before it is given to her young. They will stay together for four or five years.

Goats are members of the large family of Bovids. This means they are related to such different-looking animals as antelopes, yaks and bison. The goat has long ago been domesticated by man for its milk and hides and even for use as a draught animal for his vehicles. Nowadays, the goat is still herded in many parts of the world where its milk is made into a strong but tasty cheese. It is also kept as a pet, and the young kids can be very appealing as this picture illustrates. It is a browsing animal, but is inclined to try anything it can chew with its strong, grinding teeth, even the washing hanging on the line!

What better way to end a chapter on happy families, or a book on baby animals for that matter, than this picture of a Labrador bitch and her puppies fast asleep? There is no better sign of contentment in pets than when they sleep the sleep of utter exhaustion. The business of growing up can be tiring, as much for the mother as the youngsters. There is so much eating and exercising to be done, so many chases and fights, so many alarms and retreats, so much to learn, so much growing to be done and to be watched over. Like every family, this one has had a busy day. We can wish them all a well-earned and a quiet goodnight.

Acknowledgments

The publishers would like to thank the following individuals and organisations for their kind permission to reproduce the photographs in this book.

A.F.A. (E. H. Herbert) 105 (Geoffrey Kinns) 69; Heather Angel 88, 95; Animal Graphics 131 above; Ardea 16 (L. R. Beames) 50, 119 (T. Beamish) 54 above (D. Burgess) 44 (Clem Haagner) 77, 137 (Eric Lindgren) 51 below (E. Mickleburgh) 147 (P. Morris) 98–99 (S. Roberts) 131 below, 149 below (A. Weaving) 74–75; Bavaria Verlag 26, 31, 62 below; Camera Press Ltd 36, 63 below, 70, 85; Bruce Coleman Ltd 21, 48 above, 72, 102, 109 above and below, 111 above, 116 below (J. & D. Barlett) 102–103 (Jane Burton) 20 above and below, 23, 24–25, 114 below (Robert Burton) 90 (M. N. Boulton) 67, 148 above (A. J. Deane) 68 below (Francisco Erize) 145, endpapers (Jeff Foott) 97, 150–151 (A. R. Giddings) 138–139 (Mary Grant) 142 (David Hughes) 56 above (L. Lee Rue) 64, 73, 83 below, 93 (John Markham) 103 (J. M. Pearson) 143 (Graham Pizzey) 42 (G. D. Plage) 65, 83 above (Masood Quarishy) 75 (Hans Reinhard) 14 above, 82, 106–107, 111 below, 154 (James Simon) 86–87 (Stouffer Production) 79 (Simon Trevor) 146; Colour Library International 15, 17, 22, 60, 124, 152; James Cross 100; Anne Cumbers 18, 30 above, 37, 155; Daily Telegraph Colour Library (P. Morris) 110; Donnington Photographic 74, 78–79; Ecology Pictures (M. P. L. Fogden) 92–93 (S. Proctor) 96 (P. Ward) 38–39; Louise Hughes 12; Jacana Agence de Presse (A. Aldebert) 80–81 (Y. A. Bertrand) 134–135 (Laurent Chana) 2–3 (M. Claye) 10–11 (Devez CNRS) 46 (J. L. S. Dubois) 94 (Mouflon) 122 below (V. Renaud) 62 above (W. Schraml) 45; Frank W. Lane Photographics 63 above, 71 (Frank W. Lane) 81 (G. H. Moon) 148 below (H. Schrempp) 126–127 (Ronald Thompson) 112; Jane Miller 14 below, 128, 132 above and below, 133; John Moss 34 above, 125; Natural Science Photos 49, 114 above (C. A. Walker) 138; N.H.P.A. (D. Baglin) 104 (S. Dalton) 115, 144, 149 above (J. Good) 101 above (E. A. Janes) 113 (P. Johnson) 116 above (M. Morcombe) 41, 43 (W. J. C. Murray) 117 (P. Scott) 91 (M. W. F. Tweedie) 118 above and below (P. Wayre) 96–97 (A. G. Wells) 48 below; Oxford Scientific Films 51 above, 53, 56 below, 89 above and below, 101 below (Dr. J. A. L. Cooke) 52 above and below, 54 below 57; PAF International 84; L. Perkins 98; Pictorial Press Ltd 68 above, 108; Picturepoint Ltd 46–47, 55, 76; John Rigby 129; Spectrum Colour Library 35, 122 above, 141 above; Tony Stone Associates 34 below; Sally Anne Thompson 13, 19, 27 above and below, 28, 29 above and below, 30 below, 32 above and below, 33, 130, 140–141; John Topham Picture Library (Maurice Duris) 123 (Guy Fleury) 126 (Windridge) 120–121; Transworld Feature Syndicate Ltd 5, 66; ZEFA Picture Library 61, 136 below (W. Hamilton) 140 above (Lummer) 136 above (K. Paysan) 58–59; Zoological Society of London 40, 151, 153.